Surrounded:
Living With Islands

Collected and Edited

by Sheryl Clough

SURROUNDED: LIVING WITH ISLANDS

An Anthology by Write Wing Publishing

Clinton, Whidbey Island, Washington

Editor: Sheryl Clough

Cover Design: Constance Mears

Cover Photo: "Slea Head and Great Blasket" by Sheryl Clough

ISBN-10: 0615639933
ISBN-13: 978-0-615-63993-2

With gratitude for all those poets who have come before us, and with fond thanks to my mentor at the University of Washington, the late Professor Nelson "Moose" Bentley.

CONTENTS

Foreword: Genesis

I   EBB   1

Pamela A. Smith ... The Pier at Folly Beach   2

Sandra Ervin Adams ... Storm   3

Toni Partington ... I'm Making Time For Whitman   4

Vicki Chavis ... Currents   6

Melanie Arrowood Wilcox ... Stones in the Sand   7

William A. Carpenter ... Dutch Island Lighthouse   8

Ann Howells ... What the Witch Whispers   9

Elegy for a Small Island   10

The Waterman's Wife   11

Margo Davis ... Woman Adrift   12

II   SLACK   13

Carol Alexander ... Island   14

Margo Davis ... Walking South Point, Hawai'i   15

Ann Curran ... No Vacancies   16

Kateri Kosek ... Being So Caught Up   17

Toni Partington ... Salty Treasures   18

Sandra Marshburn ... Barrier Island   19

Ilene Adler ... Desert Island   20

Sandra Ervin Adams ... Surrender   22

Ryan Ragan ... Latitude 90   23

Constance Mears ... The Current   24

Vincent J. Tomeo ... It Rained On Easter Island   26

III FLOW   27

Teresa McElhinny ... Pressing Engagement   28

Judith O'Connell Hoyer ... Day Trip To Block Island   30

Gelia Dolcimascolo ... Solo   31

Ann Curran ... Success in Kerry   32

Ron Thompson ... Attempted Escape From An Isolated Island   33

William A. Carpenter ... Turtle Island   34

Constance Mears ... the mystic madwoman at minus tide   36

Rosemary Volz ... Ponce Inlet Mornings   37

Lois Parker Edstrom ... How Many Fathoms   38

Sheila Nickerson ... In the Broken Islands: September   39

Henry Hughes ... Making Islands   40

IV POET NOTES   43

V ABOUT THE EDITOR   48

GENESIS

What is the meaning of "island"? Human culture abounds with images and referents: Alcatraz, the Island of Dr. Moreau, "island time," Prospero's new world, Fantasy Island, Robinson Crusoe, Islands in the Stream, the Lost Continent of Atlantis. Are we oppressed, elevated, comforted or surrounded by these defined environments? Some adventurers do achieve paradise, of course. However, many of us have known people who sail away to perceived Edens, only to find themselves going stir crazy once the utopian novelty wears thin.

As though anticipating the failures of those idealists, Donne wrote "No man is an island" all those years ago, and his line has been quoted ever since. Yet iconoclasts and utopian dreamers have spent limitless energy attempting to prove him wrong. Even basic biology proves him wrong: each of us begins life as a human-created island, a miniscule clump of protoplasm confined within an inland sea.

Just as each of the twenty-four poets represented here began life as a tiny islet tethered to the main, each poem in this collection can be read as an island anchored to the literary whole, the creative entity we call a book – in which readers may float, motor, flounder or swim from one exotic shoreline to the next.

Happy Travels!

Sheryl Clough
Clinton, Washington
May 2012

Note for those intrepid islanders among you who have visited Slea Head, Ireland: the orientation of the cover photo was an artistic/design decision.

I EBB

How many ways there are of falling into the sea!

-- from "Falling" by Reuben Tam

The Pier at Folly Beach

The dolphins are not dancing today,
but the surfers sit and paddle as if
a too-tall wave may wend in any day.
And the stolid fishers ply their fishing poles
like urgent, hard-wired pick-up sticks
and set their pails in straight, attendant lanes
and fix another day's grizzled gaze,
while on the porches of the oceanfronts
small families pose, teeth gleaming,
into the horizon line where shrimpers skim.

My new doctor, the diabetes specialist, says again
that over all I'm well, hearty, nerve-alert, mostly controlled
for one so long a diabetic.
Yet, she warns, those stealth attacks, those chilling dips
into the biochemically induced netherworld,
that space which other aging Boomers might well call a trip,
may come more often
and may be tougher to be dredged up from.
Better, she chirrups, review everything, dawn to dusk, dusk to dawn.
Test, shoot, eat, test, work a little less, test and shoot again, enjoy, rest.

Best do now what's wanting to be done.

The noon sea is grey-green, Atlantic,
and no one here heeds a twit the gale warnings.
The brown thrashers flit to balconies, then bother themselves away
from our outdoor lunch nooks.
I spoon my she-crab soup, sherry-laced and peppery,
nibble salad wafers and a mound of bleu-cheesed greens.
I lemon water down my thoughts –
roughening seas and forty years on insulin.

Out beyond the pier, a solo pelican loops and circles for a quarter hour,
then plunges once, headlong,
for just what it has needed all along.

-- Pamela A. Smith

Storm

The day they closed the bridge to the island,
those who remained could not leave.
Most residents headed for mainland,
stayed with friends, or found a motel.

We stocked shelves, bought bottled water,
secured sailboat, fence, filled up with gas,
positioned generators,
covered with tarps to use later.

The enraged sea roared as evening came,
thrashed the shore of the beach.
You said if the wind blew our roof away,
we would grab the dog, crawl underneath.

That night the rock-and-roll hurricane
rumbled, and buffeted the house.
Feeder bands came and went, then the eye.
Torrents beat against the windows.

We lay motionless, waiting for morning,
the wild and wicked ocean surging.

-- Sandra Ervin Adams

I'm Making Time For Whitman

Making a space to hollow out a
perfectly shaped lemon as seeds
fall around my bare feet.

I sip black tea, push hard against the news
of Yashanee Vaughn, her body
left on Rocky Butte
in the rain, in the cold
in the leaves and grass

I'm making time for Whitman because
he knew all there was to know

I await his wisdom
answers to cloudy questions
why did sixteen-year-old Parrish Bennette Jr.
take her life; hide from her family
four agonizing months?

I'm making time for Whitman
The father I'd hoped for
            Crossing Brooklyn Ferry[1]
on his way to work, back in time for supper
            sauntering the pavement to my front door[1]
carries the news in his rumpled suit
leans over the table to ponder potatoes
two fingers in his thick, white beard
begins the story with, have you heard
we are islands, every one
it's solitude that strips our humanity

I'm making time for Whitman
to translate his lists
            camera and plate[2]
            connections of man[2]
            foot to the earth[2]
            same old law[2]
do laws keep us from harming each other, I ask

I'm making time for Whitman
     as *the spinning-girl retreats and advances to the hum of the big wheel*[3]
     as *the lunatic is carried at last to the asylum*[3]
In Portland a fist pounds a table in her grandmother's house
innocence drowned like a feral cat mid-summer
     we ask whether those who defile the living
     were as bad as they who defiled the dead?[4]

Today I make time for Yashanee Vaughn
she needs me more than Whitman
     He puts things in their attitudes[5]
     He puts today out of himself with plasticity and love[5]
     He is the answerer[5]
The mourners seek a *voice for Yashanee*[6]
she has left without final words her mother, brother, for us

Whitman said,
     Justice is not settled by legislators and laws...it is in the soul[7]
Mr. Whitman would be the first to ask,
whose soul will carry her home?

-- Toni Partington

---

[1] *Leaves of Grass, Faces*
[2] *Leaves of Grass, Song of Myself*
[3] *Leaves of Grass, Song of Myself*
[4] *I Sing the Body Electric*
[5] *Leaves of Grass, Song of the Answer*
[6] *The Oregonian,* Sunday, July 31, 2011, Sec. B
[7] *Leaves of Grass, Great are the Myths*

Currents

Mustering up conviction, I yell,
"Prepare to come about," and yank
the line taut under a darkening rim of sky,
mad at you and mad at myself.

Another spite of wind indents your features
in the sail. Snapshots pinpoint the missed years,
significant others; no anniversary pat-on-the-back
for staying in the lines of your marriage, mine.

I really get the dead eye of a caged bird,
her wings still as the doldrums,
on standby for the thrill of a breeze
to assuage her fitful, restless breast.

Suddenly windstruck, my hull drags
beneath dark water. A violent shudder
then ... release! Under a final smear
of western light, tacking hard to starboard,

I hit the wall between our parallel worlds;
it reeks of finality. Caught in the deep pull
of a rogue wave, I let go, swallowing hard;
choking on air, spitting out dreams.

-- Vicki Chavis

Stones in the Sand

We are all that remain here.
Alone together,
we are bones in sandy graves,
spirits remembered only by
simple stones in small cemeteries.

Our names are murmured by occasional visitors
carrying bags of treasure,
shells and bottles washed ashore.
They read our names,
when we were born,
and when we died.

Do they hear our voices?
I know the best places to find the conchs, the cats' paws, the scotch bonnets.
There are turtles on the north side.
…and dolphins in the inlet
if you know where to look.

They no longer hear us speaking.
We can tell them everything they want to know
and some things they'd rather not.
The storms come
carving up the Banks…

-- Melanie Arrowood Wilcox

Dutch Island Lighthouse

From Jamestown
it's a short paddle
to the point where the lighthouse stands,
a doused candle
lifting its wick to the sea.

Inside this rectangle of yellow brick
I climb stairs
that switch back along its perimeter,
a wall-clinging catwalk
thick in guano grouting.

Ascending this shaft
feels like waiting for an elevator to drop;
light filters down the flue
of this wood-and-plaster chimney
as a pigeon breaks silence
fluttering of escape.

I lift a metal trap in the ceiling
onto a metal cupola
framed with empty window panes
facing the Atlantic
where the mouth of the West Bay
gulps wind and sea.

Leaning against a rusted widow's walk,
the crow's nest of this island ship,
I watch its rocky prow break waves,
clutch the guardrail
and let the gale toss my hair
in its frothy fingers.

-- William A. Carpenter

8

What the witch whispers

Calm, green and cool,
the river enfolds our island
like a cloak. Tides
echo heartbeats.

Let me tell you, Girl,
pines hold secrets;
watch them whisper,
tremble like old women.
Listen.

I walk our land,
its perimeter. Roses,
peonies and sweet pea
gather at the gate.
This is home.

While you sleep, Girl,
music of an ebbing tide
echoes through night —
fingerings on tiny drums.
Listen.

The rutted lane
that leads away
is lost in shimmer,
a gathering of ghosts
beckons me home.

-- Ann Howells

Elegy for a Small Island

-- for JWP 1913-2006

The blue crab sheds its pinching carapace,
and salty oysters breathe blue-grey water
in the exact spot where, in a one-room school,
you day-dreamed waves. Your island,
less than one mile wide, three long, is gnawed,
silt spit into Great Shellfish Bay.

Cicadas drone a one-note dirge, dawn to dusk;
mosquitoes are roiling thunderheads.
Saltmarsh twitches with no-see-ums – ticks
and biting fleas. It gulps down wanderers,
digests their bones. Archeologists
will someday find there was an island
beneath their shallow sea; they'll display
primitive tools: dredge, seine, tongs,
ponder what forgotten deities you worshiped,
how you served them.

Nor'easters and hurricanes rage; waters rise.
You always knew water more powerful
than wind or fire, more powerful than man's
tiny constructions. Nights are black molasses.
Days are beaded glass. The river is a polished
silver plate. And, this island is sand
that trickles from a flawed hourglass.

-- Ann Howells

The Waterman's Wife

The morning river is enshrouded,
but, still, men search, emerge,
specters from the fogbank, glide,
silently pass, skiffs almost invisible.

They know time and tide,
divide the waters with imaginary lines—
Tropic of Duty, Tropic of Concern—
each searches his portion.

The boat has been found,
water-logged and foundering.
Boys pole the shallows, probe reeds
where tide has come and gone.

In the kitchen brood hens cluck,
pat hands, dish up casseroles. But,
she has been in their place, knows
the harbored relief, *it's not my man.*

She slips out, walks the shore
as mist burns off, searches for a break
in the small boats' silent gliding,
in the men's intentness.

Any coming together means
he's been found, surfaced
on this, the third day. They will try
to spare her the belly distended

as though he's feasted, the fluttering
white flesh: fingers, toes, lips fringed
and waving like anemones, eyes gone.
She won't eat crabs for months.

-- Ann Howells

Woman Adrift

Even if I kept a distance
I could smell the acrid burn, fallen leaves
within her winter frame. She stood straight among trees

overlooking the brilliant shoreline, her head hanging
like a spent beacon unable to shed any more light on
what she knew would hijack her soon enough.

Her pirated heart had floated out along
with everything else. If I approached, her inner compass
would spin out of control. No staunching this wound.

Nothing more to fall out.
She inhaled debris, her eyes flat and porous as waterlogged
planks, her thin frame so laden she ran aground.

-- Margo Davis

II SLACK

My island is a tiny dot
      not far from Sitka's shore

-- from "The Soft Rain of Sitka" by Gail Davis

Island

Let only the sea speak of islands with absolute authority.
From its boiling mad progenitors and shifting mass,
blue tongues stutter across the continental plates,
final point of the Middle Passage, feast of wicked dreams.
Here is schist and bone yard, a knuckle ground to dust.

There is pressure on this island, our footsteps on the fault.
Here we have settled on the secretive rifts, tuning our forks
to bludgeoning pitch, slapping hands, closing eyelids, making the nut,
taking shifts at dusk and dawn: islanders supping on a seismic zone.
Let only earth speak of footfalls, the high ways and the low.

Fumbling wave, tell us of islands, rust and pitted stone:
water creeping to the edge, sunken yet beneath the braided faults.
Once an ice age saw the breaching of a rock from shallow sea,
and copper figures sailed to fish from long canoes, sluicing
the waters of this estuary, this teeming island, this haunt of gulls.

-- Carol Alexander

Walking South Point, Hawai'i

The dark dog at the bottom of the hill
frightens me. Which came first, I wonder,
his lust for new blood or the choke chain
chafing his neck? By moonlight his stare
bores in from a hundred feet around my tender
flesh. My fresh droplets peering through
broken skin would glint off those ragged
bicuspids. He lunges for me, despite raw
consequence, jerking himself up on his hind legs,
his coarse bark quickening pace and pulse.
Does the sight of me, a regular unknown
so near the property, give him purpose?
Does jumping around increase his appetite?
I bet he chows down right after I turn around
at his gate, wanting the softer parts of me.

This morning I changed our routine by
striking out at dawn. The flock of wild
turkeys waddled into the thorny invasive
growth where wild pigs roam. I heard roosters
crow from the bend where the road curves
toward that dog.

                Call, then response, another crow,
differing pitches, saying many things, or
one. What do they crow about? *Good morning,*
another joyous day. Or, simply, *feed me.*

Each response echoes off-key. I round the last clump
of high trees to pair sound with sight.
My four-legged night terror has a softer side,
the pitch and echo of his crow hinting at a different
need. Perhaps each monologues the moment
the other one pauses. But on the quiet
uphill climb, I credit each with listening to
the other's need. Either way, I hear both
clearly. Then I chime in, a bit off-key,
my soft white throat exposed.

-- Margo Davis

No Vacancies

I walk past Ireland that hangs in enlarged
K-Mart glory over the stairwell
safe in darkness from morning sun that rises
in steps along the cream railings, touches
Ila's *Lion Carrousel* lithograph.

A view from the Teddy Bear House B&B
overlooking Slea Head and the Great Blasket
where we stayed, the only guests that evening,
and heard the manager tell a rowdy crowd
of hikers, *Sorry, I'm full for the night.*

-- Ann Curran

Being So Caught Up

End of summer, I watch him balance on the dory,
arms spread, one foot firm on the rim, one
held out midair. He has the boat tipped
to one side, like a child testing
the limits, braced for possible
disaster. But then, all summer
we had done this—
straddled the width
of our brief summer lives,
rocked them back and forth
to see if they would hold.

Life was dear, yes,
but we could stand to tilt too far
now and then, slip into liquid
like the seals in the bay,
the water numbing
but clear. Easier
than any conclusion.
The dory angled, tilted,
waiting to be righted. One day
while I lolled on the rocks

a seal down too long
shot to the surface
frightening me—
its deep gasp for breath,
resounding and sharp, spread
across the flatness of the bay
like a fanfare, a relief
that startled the air,
pealed conclusion.
It spluttered a few moments,
sleek head bobbing like a buoy.
We always catch ourselves just in time.

-- Kateri Kosek

Salty Treasures

what if tears turned into crystals
and everywhere they fell
lit up like northern lights

and ships at sea
once lost and alone
followed the lights to islands
stepping-stones to home

what if tears turned into diamonds
and wherever found were traded for food
so a child with swollen belly
never hungered again

what if tears turned into poems
and whenever read, struck chords
of hope in jaded hearts

and every day, no matter where
tears were considered salty treasures
flowing freely on a parched world

-- Toni Partington

Barrier Island

On a road map let your finger trace
South Carolina Highway 174 south
and run it across the Intracoastal Waterway
Bridge. Then drive your finger down
the center of Edisto Island to the Atlantic.
Dip your finger into map blue water
that runs a circle from river to ocean to river.

Drive the real road to water and sift
your fingers through sand to find sea
creatures' teeth and vertebrae.
Look for a live oak tree bent to the ground
by the 1893 hurricane and see how
it grew new trunks upright.

Walk to the mound of oyster shells
discarded by Edisto Indians. See fields
of tomatoes, beans, corn, melons,
no more rice, no more cotton.
Take a name from the phone book and trace it
to an African slave. Take another name
and trace it to an English planter. Know
that descendants of both live here.

Get a tide chart from the grocery.
Chase ghost crabs and your dog
away from sea turtle nests.
Spot a bald eagle, painted bunting.
Do not ask when drinking water will be
improved. Do not ask for fast food or hotels.

In season obey local officials who knock
on your door and tell you to evacuate.
The causeway will flood, the high bridge
will be closed due to wind. If you don't go,
wear your name on a wristband.

-- Sandra Marshburn

Desert Island

Once there was a Masai tribesman.
His face was like the parched, dry ground.
His eyes were fixed
        and though he seemed to stare,
He had been blinded by the close, hot sun.

This Masai tribesman owned a vessel.
It had been molded and baked from clay.
It was as rough as the surface
        of the cracked, lined ground
And as weathered as his sun-dried face.

The Old Man put all his faith in this vessel.
It never was out of his hand.
If it was filled with water, or milk or blood,
He would test the level with the side of his thumb
And he would know what was – or wasn't – there.

The sun scorched the wind one morning,
        as it whistled through the nervous grass.
Dry flames rushed to mark the path of the wind.
Some still say it was the shock of the heat
        that knocked the vessel from the Old Man's hand.
The hard-baked clay found the hard-baked earth
        and it shattered.
The Old Man was shattered by the sound.

The tribesman sat in the dark of the heat.
He was still sitting as the dark grew cool.
His hands cupped the memory of the vessel's shape.
One clay pot had held his view of the world.
He was besieged by all his world was not.

The tribesman sat in the dry, hot sun.
He baked like a vessel of clay.
He never spoke and made no motion for food.
Some still say they meant to counter the heat.
They filled his hands as they once had filled his cup.

The Old Man felt the shock of the water.
He tried to hold it without letting any spill.
Hot tears spilled from his two blind eyes.
The water that dripped through the bowl of his hands
        was lost to the sun-scorched ground.
The tribesman mourned because his fingers leaked.
Some still say the vessel always had.

-- Ilene Adler

Surrender

Before she passed away one Sunday
at her cottage on the beach,
my friend performed
Moonlight Sonata on her old upright.

Still, today I stand in my front yard,
living on the island
while a nor'easter roars,
my hair whipping in the wind.

Before the demon rain beats down,
I brush my hair back,
bare face and soul to the sky,
piano keys on the breeze.

-- Sandra Ervin Adams

Latitude 90

In fog, the word vapor has seven connotations.
But we're not engulfed today. Nor do we question
walking away

toward caribou ranges. Puffin, gull and mermaid
flock nearer this time, calling the chain placements.
Black stone. Volcanic bone. And here we

are. Bow-legged and drunk, cod skins hung
like coyotes over rail; our hands reaching for rudder.
It's never a matter of belonging, or having been.

Or truth. There is no telling land
to swim steadily, in place, measuring buoyancy
in waves that extend like tongues on all sides.

-- Ryan Ragan

The Current

Searchlights at the water's edge tell me
the bed check count was short,
leaving me gripping this wooden bat.
But what happens is not that thing you dread;
God invents fresh calamities
you never saw coming.
Fear swells and crests, crashing onto the futon
where I lie, soaked, shivering,
the taste of salty sweat and tears on my lips.
I strain to see form in the black night,
listen for the outline of voices,
of footsteps, of breaking glass.
Once panic wedges its toe in the door
the brain weeps like a hostage.
Most are content with metaphors of independence,
a night on the town, a solo vacation,
but my solitude is archetypal,
self-imposed exile from life
in the city. I lie here, my only hero, fully clothed,
boots on, baseball bat in hand,
counting the minutes til daybreak.

We were both hellbent on escaping:
you back to the mainland, the place from which I sought refuge.
No matter which direction you're headed
the needle on the compass quivers.
Most are content with the metaphor,
but your soul set off on this night sea journey,
you, your only hero, wooden oar in hand,
crossing a major shipping lane
in a skiff no bigger than my futon.

We both thrashed all night long,
each waking to a new horizon. You, in that busted up boat
one island over from where you were aiming.
When dawn arrived, I relaxed into the safety of light,
but my sanctuary had shifted.
Life tracks you down, like the sheriffs hauling you back
to the island. Me now adrift as you were,
the current pulling me back to the world.
This island, that island, it makes no difference.
Each day the tide pulls back the veil.
Nothing is really separate.
At minus tide we see how deep it goes—
how below the surface it's all connected,
part of one archipelago.

--Constance Mears

It Rained On Easter Island

Something there is about the rain on Easter Island

The clouds marched in like The Grand Army of The Republic
as the skies turned cotton ball white and gray
to blanket day into early evening

It rained
It poured
on Easter Island
as the Moai turned different colors
and we ran for cover over a hill into an abandoned shelter

Something there is about the rain on Easter Island
It brings life to the Moai like blood flowing through veins

We waited for the sun to come out
as the rain opened our minds to explore our thoughts
and seeds of friendship were planted forever

Something there is about the rain on Easter Island

-- Vincent J. Tomeo

III FLOW

Nearer the ocean, Sitka spruce
Grew thick in coast winds cool and moist

    -- from "The Ozette Trail" by Nelson Bentley

Pressing Engagement

I.

Can't wait to get there
    Can't seem to be there
        Shan't be late

No time to wait.
        Can't stop for chit-chat
          Can't bother with that
            Shan't slow down

No time to waste.
          My schedule is met
           My agenda is set

sorry-but-I-gotta-go-we'll-do-lunch-that-clock-is-slow-I-hear-my-page

No time to engage.

It's all so pressing, this window dressing,
ever pressed, yet seldom engaged
        spending time away
          from my cherished island home.

II.

Plenty of time to get there
    So much fun to be there
             Starting late
So we'll just wait.
        Let's all find a chair
          We'll sit over there
            Take it easy
No need for haste.
        Good to see you, friend
          So how have you been?

glad-you're-here-I-am-too-bless-your-heart-it's-time-to-start-they've-set-
    the-stage

It's time to engage.

No point in stressing, enjoy God's blessing,
seldom pressed and always engaged
        sharing time each day
          on my cherished island home.

-- Teresa McElhinny

Day Trip to Block Island

A horn bellows our leaving
and we ferry away from
the village of clamshacks,
bric-a-brac, lobster traps, bike racks.
A woman with a kerchief in her hair
cleaning plastic summer chairs
looks up as we pass her yard.
A boy stands on toothy rocks
signaling a semaphore with a stick.
He catches my eye. I wave, "Hello!"
The diesel hum muffles chatter
but for a fellow who hollers,
"Sand eels are THIS big here but
on Long Island they're THIS big!"
Clouds are borrowed
from a canvas of Narragansett
by John Frederick Kensett.
I spy a silver fish swim forth
through the painterly sky
on its way up North.
Near enough, I hear
two women head to head,
"Now Jean has a good thing…
she met a guy…the right address…
What a mess…I'm so depressed."
The ship's mascot, Cooper,
a barrel-built bulldog,
handsome, young, smug-mugged
seems fed up with the voyage.
We pass Cow Cove, Clay Head.
Old Harbor's in view.
The National still stands,
a four-tiered white belle
with black lace and widow's walk,
stale, starched, confident.
Cars zoom out of the hold.
Couples with bikes are ready to tour.
Some with maps are ready to explore
They know exactly what they want.

-- Judith O'Connell Hoyer

Solo

If I must be alone,
let me swim in water
which caresses my arms,
my torso, my legs.
Let me feel the inhale
of my own breath,
hear the gurgle
of the exhale,
the bubbling of life renewed,
to remind me
of the beginning.

-- Gelia Dolcimascolo

Success in Kerry

Great-Aunt Bridget first told me
about the grand success
of her daughter, Sarah Buckley.
She married a man with thirty cows.
He was old. Gave her one son.
The cows had their own *parlour*.
Sarah took me down to see it.
Automatic milking.
Just hook up those teats.
No more squeezing at dawn
in the damp and cold.
On that first visit, I asked
to use the bathroom.
Sarah led me to her bedroom.
Months of dust on the dresser.
She pointed to a scrub bucket.
No toilet paper nearby.

-- Ann Curran

Attempted Escape From An Isolated Island

The Intelligent Divine Designer
Assuming the IDD exists, after all,
Must be blinded or indifferent
To the fruitlessly feeble activities
Performed perfunctorily
By the absurdly comic, non-cosmic earth clowns
Like lifting off and sailing away
In a claustrophobic metal contraption
Targeted for the Moon.
And then, for them,
Only to find another earth clown
On that isolated satellite island partner,
A starving artist earth clown named Samuel Beckett,
Grotesquely squatting in a garbage bucket
30 gallon capacity
(near a tree, a shrub, a bush, a rock, a holy boot – playprop detritus).
And there he squats the Beckett in a bucket,
Obsessively wiggling
A ready-made placard scribbled in black on white:

DO NOT DISTURB UNLESS YOU ARE A GODOT NUT!

-- Ron Thompson

Turtle Island

Our ancestors roamed the seas in canoes
looking for a place to settle.
They came upon a great humped island
and beached their canoes.
It turned out to be an enormous whale
that shrugged and threw them back into the sea.
They paddled on and came to a volcano
but it turned out to be a sea serpent
that blew fire from its blowhole
and sent them back to their boats in terror.

Desperate to find land, they rowed on
to a gently sloping green hill of an island
where they made camp.
Again the land rumbled
until they realized
they were on the back of a giant sea turtle.
"Who dares trespass on my shell?" it bellowed.
The people pleaded to let them stay
for the night to regain strength for their quest.
The great turtle agreed,
but only if they caught him a meal of fish.
That evening, the people tossed
a portion of their catch to the waves
where the turtle ate at its leisure.

The next morning the turtle spoke again.
"I am old," the creature said,
"and have grown tired of my struggle for food.
You are resourceful people with your nets and fishing gear.
I will let you stay and make my back your home
if you agree to bring me fish every day before sunset."

So the people stayed
and the turtle's back grew
into a land with trees and lakes.
Other animals joined them,
they were pleased with their home.
Each evening they brought a portion of their catch
and offered it to the sea in gratitude.
And the people called the place Turtle Island.

-- William A. Carpenter

the mystic madwoman at minus tide

She sorts seaweed by stench,
fermenting a kind of coastal wisdom.
The concoction causes a raucous squawk from the gulls,
as she stockpiles fragments, bits and bones,
still hinged with life's technology.
She drags a rickety skiff across a continent of rocks
confronts the deep with her one weathered oar.
She disappears into the Mist,
but her rivets are loose and leaking;
the bay trickles into her stern.

In this Ritual of Sinking,
jumping ship is her favorite part —
a mutiny against the surface, the seduction of safety.
She sinks into the murky sea, the holy water
where shipwrecked dreams lean leeward,
creak and groan on the ocean floor.
"Mayday, mayday," she whispers to the Starfish,
patron saint of the stranded and clinging.
He reaches out with 13 arms
but she's caught in her own eddy.
She scribbles like the sea's mad secretary:
taking the moon's dictation,
dredging a rough translation of memories,
dark and eerie as eels showing up in the shadows.

She says prayers below sea level,
just to watch the cloud of bubbles
rising toward the light.
In this Ritual of Resurrection,
she ascends, breaking through the surface
with the wet bliss of a breaching whale.

-- Constance Mears

Ponce Inlet Mornings

There are no mountain dreams here,
No ghosts of Emily Dickinson
Peering out of attic windows,
No weary short-order cooks flipping
Hotcakes next to a railroad station.
This is a place of sun, and sand, and sea
And doves silhouetted against a restless sky
As gulls practice their screeching song
And ghost-crabs live or die at the
Sovereign good pleasure of the tides.

Here old men bait hooks,
Young men wax boards,
And a lonely woman looking for weeds
Finds some grace and mercy instead.
This is a place of beginnings and endings
With no great expectations in the middle.
Here we dream of photographs on the wall
And write our histories on the wind.
Here we throw salt on time and loneliness
And force old bones to greet the sun.

All wake with the same hunger.
All want a little coffee and joy before death.
And when white sheets turn and bay trees rustle,
We want to be in a place near familiar
Where the heart is still but the spirit dances,
Where we are gently rooted to a watery place
As wild as a tempest, as peaceful as home.

-- Rosemary Volz

How Many Fathoms*

Saturday night and cruise ships sail past
my window, horizontal skyscrapers lit to rival
the aurora borealis, through Admiralty Inlet,
the Straits of Juan de Fuca, out to open sea.

Like grey whales migrating north
to summer feeding, I watch them go,
island-grounded by the heliotrope
I planted today, the goldfinch poised

in the white lilac, a small brown rabbit
that lives under my doorstep. Here
the red-tailed hawk ignites a flame
of sunlight and herons hunker in the fields.

I return to the wild rose thicket again
and again, gild my nose with pollen.
No matter how greedy I am
I cannot deplete the scent.

-- Lois Parker Edstrom

---

*Originally published in *Soundings Review*, September 2009.

In the Broken Islands: September

A friend kayaks in the Broken Islands.
Here, on autumn's beach,
trees exchange green flags for red
and outside furniture is put away.
Each shore becomes more
separate and distant.

Let whales and sea stars protect
her. Let the archipelago stretch
out its long rocky arms
and waves be gentle
as a lover's hands,
guiding her in.
I have so much to tell her.

-- Sheila Nickerson

Making Islands

1.

Tongues
brashing like dolphins,
we stroke
warm seams
and swells,
diving to the bed.

Depth can be scary—
twisted wrecks, whale bones, dark rifts
and currents. But we want it, unzipping,
hipping over hot vents, moaning
each surging stroke. Our luscious
cones swirl and blow,

and the island rises—
steam, smoke, fire and flow.
Glowing rivers
cooling shoulders
into sleep.

2.

Over the years
love hardens, ripens
and grows soft again. Gardens sway,
while our children play
in the sunny sand,
then sail away
with people we hardly know.

Sun setting easy and rising slow,
we hope nothing
erupts on the horizon
or washes up
to be saved.
Rocks say we're sinking. That's okay.
The earth makes beautiful things
and takes them away.

-- Henry Hughes

IV POET NOTES

But I was only a poet – that is to say, a maker of stone axes
  – and she felt a real pity for me because of it ...

  -- from *Pictures From An Institution*, Randall Jarrell

Sandra Ervin Adams is listed in *A Dictionary of American Poets & Writers* and has been published in anthologies and literary journals. In 2006 she authored a poetry chapbook, *Union Park Poems*, and another in 2011, *Through a Weymouth Window*. She lives near the North Carolina Coast.

Ilene Adler teaches English as a Second Language at a Japanese cultural center and is writing a memoir titled "How I Changed My Mind." Currently, she is in a writing class taught by Mindy Lewis, author of "Life Inside" which is run by the Writer's Voice in New York City.

Carol Alexander's poetry appears in *Avocet, Boyne Berries* (UK), *Chiron Review, Cave Moon Press, The Canary, Danse Macabre, Earthspeak, Fade Poetry Journal* (UK), *Fat Daddy's Farm Press, The Mad Hatter's Review, Mobius, Numinous, OVS, Red Poppy Review, Red River Review, River Poets Journal, Sleeping Cat Books,* and *The Whistling Fire.*

William A. Carpenter's poetry has appeared in *Runes, Blueline, Chest, Balancing the Tides, July Literary Press* and the *RI Writer's Circle Anthology*. He is a member of the Ocean State Poets, whose mission is to bring poetry and give voice to divergent populations, such as prisoners and children at risk.

A working writer living in Fort Myers, Florida, Vicki Chavis is an award-winning poet, freelance editor and writer, blogger and foodie. She is currently writing a book about PTSD and how she survived an "unsurvivable" plane crash.

Ann Curran, author of *Placement Test,* a book of poems, hails from Pittsburgh, PA. She holds both U.S. and Irish citizenship. Her poetry appears in *Rosebud Magazine, U.S. 1 Worksheets, Notre Dame Magazine, Ireland of the Welcomes, Commonweal* and others. She has worked as a journalist, freelance writer, and magazine editor.

Margo Davis lives in Houston. Over the years her poems have appeared in *Louisiana Literature, Texas Poetry Calendar, The New Orleans Review, Ellipsis, Maple Leaf Rag* and *Passages North*. She received two honorable mentions, the *Billie Stroud Appreciation Award* and Houston's *Robert Clark Appreciation Award.*

An award-winning poet with a BA in Fine Arts from the University of California, Irvine, Gelia Dolcimascolo has been a Writing Tutor and *The Writers' Circle* facilitator for 23 years at Georgia Perimeter College. Her poems appeared in numerous publications, including *Haiku Pix Review* and *Poetry of the Golden Generation.*

Lois Parker Edstrom's poetry has appeared in *Birmingham Arts Journal, Borderlands, Floating Bridge Review,* and *Connecticut River Review.* Her chapbook *What Brings Us to Water* received the Poetica Publishing Company Chapbook Award in 2010. Her second collection, *What's To Be Done With Beauty,* is forthcoming from Creative Justice Press. Lois lives on Whidbey Island, Washington.

Ann Howells has edited Dallas Poets Community's journal, *Ilya's Honey,* for thirteen years. Her chapbook, *Black Crow in Flight,* was published by Main Street Rag. She has two Pushcart nominations and one Best of the Web nomination. Her work most recently appeared in *Borderlands, Calyx, Cenzio, RiverSedge,* and *Spillway.*

Judith O'Connell Hoyer is a retired school psychologist and special education director who has abandoned knitting, housework and shopping in the pursuit of poetry – reading it and writing it. She is active in several Boston area poetry groups and has been published in *The Yale Journal for Humanities in Medicine.*

Henry Hughes grew up on Long Island, New York and now lives in Falls City, Oregon. His three collections of poetry include *Men Holding Eggs,* which received the 2004 Oregon Book Award. He is the editor of the Everyman's Library anthology, *The Art of Angling: Poems about Fishing.*

Kateri Kosek holds a BA from Vassar and an MFA from Western Connecticut State University, where she also mentors graduate students. Her poetry has appeared in *Orion, Crab Orchard Review,* and *Rhino,* and her essays have been published in *Creative Nonfiction, Blueline,* and *Terrain.org.*

Sandra Marshburn's poems have appeared in various journals, anthologies and four chapbooks; the most recent, *Telling Time,* from March Street Press. She taught at West Virginia State University for a number of years and now resides on Edisto Island, South Carolina.

During her single years, Teresa McElhinny was a journalist/ editor/scriptwriter in the Philippine Islands. She moved with her husband and 14-year-old son to Whidbey Island in 2007. She is active within Whidbey Island Writers Association and is working on a series of character-driven short stories involving the same female protagonist.

Constance Mears first got lost in the world of poetry at age 11. These poems were written during the two plus years she lived in solitude on Cypress Island. An artist, writer and mystic, she is currently working on a spiritual memoir.

Sheila Nickerson is a former resident of Juneau and Poet Laureate of Alaska. Her work has been widely published in magazines, anthologies, and chapbooks and has received two Pushcart Prizes. Her nonfiction includes *Disappearance: A Map* and *Midnight to the North: The Untold Story of the Inuit Woman Who Saved the* Polaris *Expedition.*

Toni Partington is a poet, editor, and visual artist based in Vancouver, Washington. She is the author of two poetry books, *Jesus Is A Gas* (2009) and *Wind Wing* (2010). She is Co-Editor for *VoiceCatcher* and co-founder and editor of Printed Matter Vancouver, an editing and small press service.

Ryan Ragan's work has appeared in *Cutbank, Spillway, Booth,* and *Apple Valley Review.* His writing has been nominated for Best New Poets 2011 and Best of the Net 2011. He is the poetry editor of the journal *Permafrost* at the University of Alaska Fairbanks and is an MFA candidate there.

Pamela A. Smith is an educator, administrator, and author of ten books. Her poems and articles have appeared in literary and religious journals and collections for several decades. She has been a Type 1 diabetic for 42 years.

Ron Thompson is a caregiver, an assistant to people with the perplexities of a disabled life. Experimental artist and writer, his play "The Abrupt Edge of Reality" involved a cast of dozens and played to a rowdy SRO crowd. He continues to boldly attempt gardening in the foothills of Washington's Cascade Mountains.

Vincent J. Tomeo has been published in the *New York Times, Comstock Review, Mid-America Poetry Review, Spires, Tiger's Eye, ByLine, Mudfish, The Blind Man's Rainbow, Edgz, The Neovictorian/Cochlea, The Latin Staff Review* and *Grandmother Earth (VII-XI).* His poems have won numerous awards.

Born in Brooklyn, Rosemary Volz graduated *summa cum laude* from Queens College, where she won numerous awards, including the Presidential Achiever's Award. Her short stories have been published in *Blueline, Event, Another Chicago Magazine* and *Reader's Choice.* She is associated with the Tomoka Poets and lives in Ponce Inlet, Florida.

Melanie Arrowood Wilcox is writing a creative nonfiction history of Portsmouth Island, North Carolina. Portsmouth, adjacent to Ocracoke Island, is an abandoned village that was most prosperous during the 1800s. It is now part of Cape Lookout National Seashore.

V ABOUT THE EDITOR

After several years in Alaska, where she obtained her MFA in Creative Writing, Sheryl Clough returned to her native Puget Sound, eventually settling on Whidbey Island. Sheryl has worked as a paralegal, naturalist, whitewater river guide, Upward Bound teacher, and instructor of composition and literature at Highline College. She currently owns and operates Write Wing Publishing, a writing/editing/proofreading service and small publishing house. Recent honors include a creative nonfiction prize from Jane's Stories Press Foundation and the William Stafford Award from Washington Poets Association.

Sheryl blogs at: www.scatchetpoet.blogspot.com.

www.ingramcontent.com/pod-product-compliance
Lightning Source LLC
Chambersburg PA
CBHW021914040426
42447CB00007B/855